How to Use Symbol and Action in Worship

John Leach

Parish Development Adviser,

Diocese of Monmouth, Church in Wales

GROVE BOOKS LIMITED

RIDLEY HALL RD CAMBRIDGE CB3 9HU

Contents

The Cover Illustration is by Peter Ashton

Acknowledgments

Thanks to Mark Earey, Ian Tarrant and others from GROW for your help and advice. And thanks to Peter for all you have taught me and the fun I had learning it.

First Impression August 2005
ISSN 0144-1728
ISBN 1 85174 598 X

Introduction: Worship Beyond Words

We were in the sports hall of the University of Kent at an international conference for over 800 Anglican church leaders from around the world. I had been a part of the team planning the worship for the conference, and we had decided that each day we would use the communion liturgy from one of the provinces of the Anglican communion. Today was the Church of South India, and before the service (for which we had been requested to remove our shoes, as Indian Christians would) I was browsing the service booklet. I noticed a rubric which said that at the Offertory 'gifts of flowers may be offered in thanks for God's creation.' I wondered whether we would do that, and if so how.

At the offertory, while we were singing an Indian-style worship song, I became aware of some Indian women, dressed in beautifully coloured saris, entering from the back of the hall carrying trays loaded high with flower petals. They processed to the front and began to sprinkle the altar, the eucharistic vessels, the bishop who was presiding at communion, the musicians and just about everything else with petals. I found myself inexplicably sobbing like a baby at the sheer beauty of the moment, and talking to others afterwards I had not been alone in this reaction. To this day I cannot tell you what I was crying about, but merely that it was a very powerful spiritual moment.

This story could be told in many ways and with many variations by many in the church today. It seems to be an observable fact that people increasingly are meeting God as much through what is *done* in worship as through what is said, sung or heard. Many churches are realizing the value of symbol and action in worship, and are seeking in different ways to make use of it. This book is intended to provide a simple guide to churches wanting to move into this area, and to set out a process which can be helpful in planning and using symbol and action. Along the way are some questions for discussion—you may like to use them with a church council or worship planning group, rather than just reading through this book on your own. The hope is, of course, that your discussion will result in action.

Many churches are realizing the value of symbol and action in worship

If you want some theoretical background to this subject, I can point you to no more helpful book than Peter Craig-Wild's *Tools for Transformation*[1]. His argument briefly is that the Enlightenment science-based culture through which we have lived for the past few hundred years has conditioned the church into some assumptions, particularly about the superiority of words. It is noticeable that when Christians from what you might call 'liturgical churches' want to renew or move on their worship, they do so by producing new books full of different words. We have spent immense amounts of committee time and money working solely on new words, believing that church renewal would result. This tendency, present in many branches of the church, has led to what Peter calls 'one-dimensional worship,' which works with a set of Enlightenment-based presuppositions:

- Mind is better than body
- Conscious is better than unconscious
- Individual is better than community
- Reason is better than emotion
- Precision is better than ambiguity
- Fact is better than feeling
- Truth is better than mystery

But now culture has moved on, these presuppositions are being questioned, and many people, including (incidentally) non-Christians, are seeking a spirituality based more on what we *do* and *feel* than on theological certainties pinned to the dissecting board by words.

I am not, of course, wanting to set up a dichotomy between words and symbols, or to say that symbols are good and words are bad. Words are still very useful things, and I am not suggesting that they now need replacing. What I am wanting, though, is to help the church redress the balance and realize that it is possible to meet God beyond words as well as through them.

For Discussion

What do we regularly do in our worship which does not involve words at all, or which uses words only incidentally?

How do you think people feel about these elements in our worship?

Why Symbol and Action?

Before we embark on the 'how to' section which will form the bulk of this book, it is worth pausing briefly to ask why we should bother with this subject. I want to suggest five reasons.

Because of Who God Is

It seems to be an embarrassing fact for those with a bit of a puritan streak in them that the God revealed in Scripture seems to revel in symbol, imagery, colour and action. The sheer variety of the created world, the way he required worship to be offered, the imagery and symbolism through which he called his prophets to speak to his people—all these point to a God for whom the sensory was at least as important as the verbal and intellectual. And lest we feel tempted to write all this off as 'Old Testament,' we only have to look at Jesus, who healed through spit and mud, set people free from evil with pigs as a visual aid, who used water for baptism and bread and wine for communion. Symbolism is risky, of course; it works precisely because it lacks the precision of words, and is open to all kinds of misunderstanding and misuse[2]. But it appears to be the case that even with the possibility of us getting it wrong, God chooses to take the risk anyway.

Because of Who We Are

The fact that God chooses to communicate beyond words suggests that humans are capable of hearing him beyond words. Now that we have become familiar with various systems of personality typing we are more aware that in any given group of people there will be a mixture of those who prefer to work, worship and learn in different ways. Myers-Briggs dominant 'S' people, and Cognitive Styles Analysis 'Imagers' are just two groups of people whom the church has sold short where it has placed exclusive emphasis on words.

> *The fact that God chooses to communicate beyond words suggests that humans are capable of hearing him beyond words*

Because of How Old We Are

Another good reason for using symbol and action in worship is that it can be very all-age-friendly. My wife was recently speaking at an all-age service in a pretty traditional rural parish which, through its significant involvement in a current community issue, had seen a sudden influx of young families. The village school had been under threat of closure, and church members had campaigned vigorously against it, such that the school decided to back the church just as they felt the church had backed them. Easter Sunday saw about 50 extra children and their families in church. As I write this attendance is continuing.

The theme for the day was the Emmaus Road story, and Chris decided that her aim was to encourage people to become more aware of the presence of Jesus with them in their everyday lives, perhaps where they had previously been unaware of it. After her talk everyone was given a cut-out footprint, and encouraged to write or draw on it a situation or place where they had come to realize that Jesus had been present with them all along. From now on they would seek to be more aware of him. A long roll of stone-coloured wallpaper was laid down the central aisle of the church, and people were encouraged to Pritt-stick their footprint onto this 'road,' with a prayer for the presence of Jesus to go with them. What was encouraging in clearing up afterwards was the variety of responses, from 'at my playgroup' to 'in my greenhouse' and 'when I'm driving on dark roads at night.' These kinds of responses suggest a true all-age accessibility. It truly had been an all-age service rather than just a 'children's service.'

These kinds of responses suggest a true all-age accessibility

Because of How the World Is

We have already noted that the emerging post-postmodern culture will be one where the dry sterility of the scientific and technological approach to life is replaced by a much more touchy-feely character, where the way something feels to me will become much more important than whether someone else thinks they have proved it to be objectively true. The challenge for Christians is to present eternal and changeless truths in ways which will enable them to be heard and understood in a world where image and impact are much more important than truth and precision. Helping people to experience God rather than merely theorizing about him will be key in twenty-first century evangelism.

Helping people to experience God rather than merely theorizing about him will be key in 21st Century evangelism

Because of How You Are

I have taught widely around Britain on this subject, and without exception my audiences have instantly recognized and accepted what I am saying. People have been able to tell me stories of encounters with God through more than just words, and in many churches people are feeling their way towards a more action-based worship style and are experimenting with the kinds of things we shall be discussing in this book. I believe the church is ready for this, and that God is actively putting symbol and action on our agenda to redress the balance.

For Discussion

Think for a moment about any times when you would say you have met with God 'beyond words.' Could you share one or two of these experiences with the group?

So, how might we begin to join in with what God is doing and give action and symbol their rightful place in the worship of his people?

3

The Backdrop— Creating Atmosphere

Before we begin to think about what we might do in a worship setting, let us pause to consider what impression our worship-space might have on us as we enter it.

The impact on our five senses will affect how we are able to worship and encounter God, before we do anything at all in 'the service' itself. Liturgists talk of 'transitions' into worship, and the way we help people into the presence of God at the start of worship can be vitally important.

For Discussion

Imagine I came to your church next Sunday for your normal service. As I walked in, what would I—

- See?

- Hear?

- Feel? (I do not mean emotionally, I mean physically)

- Smell?

- Taste?

I have asked people these questions many times, and I have received a variety of answers, many of them sadly rather negative. I then go on to ask the supplementary:

- What impression would all the above have on me as I came to worship?

So how might we set out to engage the five senses as a backdrop for worship?

Sight

How might you enhance the visual impact of your worship-space? Use of liturgical colours, not just at the front but throughout the building, can help create an appropriate atmosphere. So can lighting. Peter Craig-Wild tells in his book of a church which spent tens of thousands on a reordering scheme but saved a few hundred pounds by having light switches rather than dimmers. The lighting could only ever be on or off. One year Peter lit his church during Holy Week simply from two OHPs with coloured acetates thrown up against the walls; all the other lights were turned off altogether. Many churches will use banners or other fabrics, which can add a bit of 'soft furnishing' to the hard stone and wood of the building. And increasingly churches whose architecture permits will use images or even the notices for the week via OHP or a PowerPoint loop as a preparation for worship. Candles, icons and the like have also been used traditionally in some churches to aid devotion.

Sound

If your church prepares for worship with noisy chatter or a band tuning up or practising you might like to think about what could more helpfully lead people into an atmosphere of worship. I often hear of a tension between those who see this time as the family gathering, for chattering and catching up, and those who want reverent silence or quiet organ music to prepare for worship. This is a common tension. One way round it is for the service leader to come out and give the welcome and notices a couple of minutes before the service begins, and for there to be a period of quiet from then until the ministers enter for worship itself. Some churches make use of recorded music before the service, while in others the organist or worship band play appropriate music.

Feeling

I am not talking here about emotions like boredom or excitement, but rather the physical feel of the building. Most people I ask tell me that in their church I would feel hard wood and cold radiators. Those who are not blessed with upholstered chairs have got a problem on their hands, although there are ways to help make the seats a bit more hospitable. Temperature is important too, and as well as the more normal cold of church buildings it is also possible for them to be airless and stuffy. Neither of these will enhance a sense of welcome to worship.[3]

Smell

'Mould' and 'damp' are the most common responses to my question in this category. Even if your church in not renowned for its incense-swinging, there are still some things you can do. Incense might be used in preparation for rather than during the service. In my experience most of those who object to it do so not on the grounds of the aroma but on the behaviour of the thurifer. I used to fill my church with smoke a couple of hours before special services like Midnight at Christmas so that by the time the service started the smell was lingering but the clouds of smoke were not. People generally found this evocative without being offensive. I also know of churches which put the coffee for the end of the service on to brew before it starts, and even some which use a carefully-timed breadmaker at the back of church to prepare the bread for the communion.

Taste

This is perhaps the most neglected of the senses, but as we shall see there is much which can be done to engage people here, certainly during if not before the service. The bread and wine, of course, engage our sense of taste, as do decent coffee and even doughnuts after the service or during a coffee break

Churches are increasingly serving coffee before the service, since this helps to include newcomers and visitors before worship begins

between the Liturgies of Word and Sacrament, forming a kind of extended Peace. Churches are increasingly serving coffee before rather than (or as well as) after the service, since this helps to include newcomers and visitors before worship begins.

These issues of background and atmosphere are important, since they prepare the worshippers for what is to come. In the mid-seventies, (between Series 2 and Series 3, for any liturgical anoraks) English Anglicans dropped the words 'into the world' from the post-communion prayer of sending out—since then we have prayed simply 'Send us out in the power of your Spirit...' Whilst this recognition that we do not come out of the world to church and therefore

People are coming to holy space for a period of time set aside for their attention to be focussed on God

need to re-enter it at the end is a good one, it is nevertheless important to help people recognize that what they do as they come to worship is different from their everyday lives. They are coming to holy space for a period of time set aside for their attention to be focussed on God. Anything we can do to mark out this time and space as different and holy will be a helpful aid to worship.

For Discussion

Is there one thing, inspired by thinking through these questions of background and atmosphere, which we could do differently, starting next week, which would be non-controversial? Will we do it?

Using Symbol and Action
— A Checklist

4

I am the kind of person who likes detailed lists of instructions which work logically through the task and leave me very little room to get things wrong (although I still manage to!).

One of my favourite tasks is assembling flat pack furniture, using those cute little Swedish drawings. Is it possible to provide such logical and idiot-proof instructions for using symbol and action in worship? It is my intention to try in this next section, although sadly and ironically in a book about symbols I will need to do it with words. Then in case you still managed to get it wrong I will end with a section on how not to do it.

Where Might It Help?

At what point in the flow of the service might we want to *do* something? Some suggestions might be:

- Before the service starts
- As an opening activity
- Around the penitential section
- In response to God's word
- During or after communion
- At the end or after the service

Of course this is not an exhaustive list, merely a few suggestions. The real question, given the liturgical shape and the theme and teaching aims for the service, is 'What might help people to understand and respond to what God is saying to them today?' Where would *doing* something help people to understand better or experience more deeply the grace of God?

Where would doing something help people to understand better or experience more deeply the grace of God?

To help us understand this more fully, let us work through a specific example.
You have decided this week to emphasize the penitential part of the service
(perhaps it is the first Sunday of Lent or Advent). Instead of just saying a
prayer of confession, you want to allow people more space to deal with sin
and repentance. So how do we begin to think beyond words?

What Does the Bible Say?

A good starting point is to explore what the Bible has to say on the subject.
There are many different images and pictures for sin, repentance and forgiveness in the pages of Scripture. These would include:

- Darkness and light/day and night
- Sin as pollution or stain
- Slavery to sin
- The burden of sin
- Dead in sin/alive in Christ
- Enmity/friendship with God
- Sins of habit
- Broken relationships
- Exclusion
- Hardheartedness
- Separation

and so on. There is a rich variety of symbol available without going any further
than the pages of the Bible.

What Could People Do?

Given all these possibilities, is there anything which people could do in turning
the Bible's images or metaphors into action? Two examples spring to mind,
neither of which has to do with penitence, but both of which take the Bible
at face value. The first was at a retreat in which Peter and I were involved
for several hundred church leaders from around the world, mainly Anglican
bishops who were assembling for the Lambeth Conference in Canterbury.
We were aware that as they gathered many would be worn out from days of
journeying, and some would have left their churches and people in situations
of hardship, famine, warfare or persecution. They were coming to a strange

culture and a foreign land, perhaps for the first time. Our aim was to prepare them for the main conference with some spiritual tender loving care.

The retreat began with the people sat around tables in groups of eight or so. In the middle of each table was a bowl of dry sand, and we invited them to run their hands through the sand to see if it reflected in any way how they felt—dry, dusty, gritty. Perhaps it spoke to them of their homelands, or the situations they had left behind. Then, against gentle background music, someone read from Isaiah 35, about the desert rejoicing and blossoming. As the passage was being read, people moved among the tables and handed each leader a flower, as both a prayer and a promise for the days which lay ahead. It was a beautiful way to begin the retreat, and the surprise value had many people deeply moved. What had we actually done? We had turned the Bible's metaphor into action—if the desert was going to blossom, let us get some sand and flowers. It is not rocket science, but it set the scene beautifully for what turned out to be an excellent few days.

We had turned the Bible's metaphor into action—if the desert was going to blossom, let us get some sand and flowers

Slightly nearer to home, we were celebrating Harvest festival in the church I used to lead. People turned up as usual and sat in the pews, but the service began with me telling everyone to get up and go over to the church hall next door. When they walked in they saw right along the middle of the hall a line of tables which were laden with piles and piles of fresh fruit of every type and colour you can imagine. A member of the congregation who was a market gardener had donated the food, which had then been cut up and beautifully arranged. I simply told people to 'Taste and see that the Lord is good' and for the next 15 minutes we feasted on the bounty of God's provision both with our mouths and our eyes. When we returned to the church for the rest of the service, the worship flew! Again, we had turned a picture or metaphor into action by tasting and seeing.

When we returned to the church for the rest of the service, the worship flew!

So how might we *do* penitence in the light of the biblical images? In all sorts of ways, but first there is another question to be asked.

What Might People Do?

As soon as you begin to think biblically about action in terms like these, you become aware of one fact—biblical worship was messy. We could in theory cut up a goat or two during the penitential section. (In fact we *nearly* cut up a toy sheep, Sean from *Wallace and Grommit*, at the start of an all-age service on one occasion, but the service leader explained just in the nick of time as the axe was about to fall that because Jesus had died we no longer needed that kind of sacrifice any more, and we could come to worship through him. We had a time of ministry for terrified children at the end.) We might throw gallons and gallons of water around the church, or upend a huge jug of oil over someone. But we probably would not get away with it. Peter Craig-Wild points out the way in which nowadays Anglicans in particular have sanitized our symbols. A little drip of water, a tiny sip of wine, a neatly cut cube of Hovis, and an oily thumbprint are about all we are likely to get nowadays. What a contrast with the sheer mess of biblical worship! Rightly or wrongly, though, and I think a lot of it has to do with living in an indoors kind of climate, our wildest and most literal biblical interpretations are not going to help anyone if they are so outrageous that people will not join in, or if we have irate churchwardens after us because the church needs recarpeting. So without dumbing things down too much, we do need to make our worship accessible to people.

Without dumbing things down too much, we do need to make our worship accessible to people

Again, here are two examples, one from Peter and one from me. At the start of a service everyone in the congregation was given a 20cm length of wool. What colour? Scarlet, of course. We were invited to meditate on those things for which we particularly needed forgiveness, and on the blood of Christ which had bought it for us. Then a long length of rope was passed around the congregation, snaking along the rows and over people's heads. We were invited to tie our bit of wool onto the rope, which was finally draped around a large rough wooden cross at the front, forming a beautiful picture for the rest of the service of the power of the cross and Jesus blood to take away sin.

On another occasion I was preaching about sins of habit, those little things which we could stop any time but which gradually gripped and enslaved us without our realizing. As I was speaking two other people began to walk round and round me, winding thin red wool round me and trapping my arms. It was obvious that at any time I could have raised my arms and snapped the wool, but the longer I stood passively and let them do it, the more the wool bound me up, to the point where escape would have been very difficult indeed. Then, as the absolution was given, the wool was unwound and I was free.

So we decide where we might fit in some symbol or action, ask about biblical images, and decide whether there might be anything we could get people to do which flowed from Scripture but would not be too offensive.

Having decided what you think you might like to do, the next stage is to think through a series of practical questions.

What Will We Need?

I was speaking at a service in Yorkshire on Advent Sunday. We decided that we wanted to focus on a 'past and future' theme. The bread and wine of the communion would take us back to what Jesus had done on the cross for us in a past historical event, but we wanted something to help us look forward to our destination. We decided to invite people to take milk and honey after having taken bread and wine, a biblical symbol of the Promised Land to which God's people are journeying, and another use of our most neglected sense, taste. But then the real hard work began. How would we actually do it?

The milk was not too difficult—some little plastic cups did the trick. But what about honey? If I had had my own way I would have just got a large bowl and invited people to roll up their sleeves like Samson and dig in, but there is probably some health and safety regulation against that. We thought tea-spoons were a bit much, and decided that what we really needed was those little stirring sticks you get at McDonalds. But due to our failure to plan very far in advance, we were not sure where we could get 250 McDonalds-style stir-sticks at 9 pm on a Saturday evening. One possible answer would of course have been McDonalds, but frankly we did not really have the nerve to go and ask. But we did find a pack of drinking straws which, when cut into thirds, did the trick beautifully. But then we thought on. Where would people get their straws? A little plate was needed to put them on. And once they had sucked honey off them, where would they go then? Another bowl or plate was required for the used ones. In fact the service worked very well in the end, but failure to think through all these minute details and provide everything which was needed would have caused all sorts of difficulties which would have diverted the attention from God onto the symbols which were only there to speak of him.

Failure to think through all these minute details would have caused all sorts of difficulties which would have diverted the attention from God

Another equipment question, and another example of the sense of taste, came out of an all-age Good Friday meditation. In thinking about the service beforehand I had been particularly struck by the incident of the offering of vinegar to Jesus to drink. That must surely have been just about the last straw for Jesus. Even in the middle of so much agony and suffering he couldn't even get a simple drink of water to slake his thirst—they gave him something even more bitter than his pain. This seemed to me a powerful symbol of human cruelty and mercilessness at its most extreme, the kind of cruelty which in fact had sent him to the cross in the first place. In response to a meditation around this theme I decided it would be good to invite people forward to sip some vinegar, using a different sense to experience just a small taste of Jesus' suffering for them.

My initial plan was to fill a chalice with vinegar and invite people to sip from it, but I was not sure about the hygiene of this, and in any case Jesus had received his vinegar from the end of a stick. So in the end we used a packet of cotton buds which people dipped into the vinegar and then sucked. Again we needed somewhere for the clean and used sticks to go.

A related question which needs thinking through will be…

How Will It Work?

If your building is spacious and airy you are fortunate indeed, but many of us have to worship in a confined space almost every square inch of which is littered with Victorian woodwork and/or worship band clutter. If we are asking people to move anywhere during the service, we will need to have thought through the logistics if we are to avoid unseemly traffic jams or near misses like those motorcycle displays at the Royal Tournament.

One Pentecost I was preaching on the empowering of the Holy Spirit for mission, and I decided with the vicar that we would offer people a range of possible responses. First of all they could come forward to receive bread and wine as usual. The emphasis here was on the objective fact of what Jesus had done for us. But of course we needed to respond, so after taking communion people were invited to move to the font, which would be open and full of water. This spoke of their personal response, through baptism, to what Jesus had done, and people were invited to spend a moment remaking their baptism commitment to serve Jesus, and perhaps using some water on their hands or forehead to remember those promises and reinforce them. But the third stage, which Pentecost is all about, is our need for the anointing of the Spirit to empower us for

Clearly this could have been a recipe for disaster, so we carefully arranged things so that there was a kind of one-way system

Jesus' service, so we had another two stations where people could go and receive anointing with oil and prayer to be filled or refilled with the Spirit. Clearly this could have been a recipe for disaster, so we carefully arranged things (not that we could do much arranging with the font or the communion rail) so that there was a kind of one-way system, which we asked people to observe in order to maintain a reverent atmosphere.

How Will It Be Announced?

When I was a student I was invited to a friend's church to hear a famous speaker who had a high-profile ministry in a particular African country. The talk was both interesting and inspiring, and at the end there was the inevitable appeal. 'Is God calling you to serve him in Africa?' We had heard about the terrible needs and the golden opportunities, and now it was time to recruit more workers into the vineyard. We were invited to stand, and a few people did, but that clearly was not enough, as the speaker continued, with increasing volume, to call us to a response. The appeal took almost as long as the sermon had done, and in the end I guess about a third of the 250 or so people present were on their feet.

Even then I must have been something of a cynic, because I remember questioning to myself whether God was *really* calling that many people to one small African country *from Nottingham*. What about Leicester, or Scunthorpe? Africa was in danger of sinking under the weight if he had this much success at every evening of his UK tour.

The question of manipulation in worship is nowhere more significant than in the area we are considering in this book. We want at all costs to avoid two mistakes: getting people to do what we want them to out of a sense of guilt or conformity when their hearts are not actually in it; and putting people's backs up so they will not respond on principle whatever we ask them to do.

I have written elsewhere on handling response,[4] so I will not repeat that material here, but suffice to say that leaders of worship should allow a range of possible options—indeed one definition of manipulation is 'allowing only one possible acceptable response.' In my Pentecost example above I invited people to do any, all or none of the three activities as they felt they wanted to respond to God. I also try always to create a culture where *not* responding is as valid as responding, so that there is no felt pressure. I usually preface my comments with 'This will not be for everyone, but there may be a few of you who feel you would like to...' whatever it is. At the end of the day, it is counterproductive to force a response—what we want, surely, is for those to whom the Spirit is speaking to respond, and those to whom he is not to sit and pray quietly for the others.

This non-manipulative approach is essential in all-age or children's settings. On one occasion my wife was taking her Kidz Club group (consisting mainly of non-churched children) through a series on the Ten Commandments. Week three, as you might expect, was about using God's name thoughtlessly, and her teaching input was about the way in which nowadays everyone says 'O God' virtually all the time, and how would they feel if people used their names like that?

She went on to explain that in the past children who were heard by their parents saying rude words were sent to wash their mouths out. It may be, she went on, that after today you have realized that you sometimes say things like that, or use God's name wrongly. You may not have noticed before now, because no-one may have told you it was wrong, but now you may have come to realize how much it upsets God, and you would like not to do it again.

At the front were some cups of diluted mouthwash and a large bucket. Any child who felt they wanted to could come forward to wash their mouths out, and spit it out into the bucket. But you should only do it, Chris told them, if you have felt God speaking to you, and not just because others were doing it, or because you thought it would be fun to spit in church. You might think this would have been a recipe for great hilarity, but in fact many of the children did come forward, and there was a sense of the profound presence of the Spirit of God, with no silliness and all the spitting directed exclusively into the bucket. The way that it had been set up and announced ensured that only those who wanted to take it seriously would actually do it.

It is worth mentioning here another aspect of announcing symbolic action—the relationship between word and symbol. I said at the start that I do not want to suggest that words are bad and symbols are good, but there is a complex relationship between them which is worth pausing to consider. Liturgist Mark Earey talks about three possible uses of words and symbols. Take the simple act of lighting a candle. Firstly it may be lit with the words 'We light this candle to remind us that Jesus is the light of the world.' This is *explanation*—words are being used to tell us why we are using a certain action, and what it means. The symbol adds to the words, but does not take them any further.

Secondly the candle may be lit with the words 'Jesus is the light of the world.' Here the words are not exactly explaining why we are doing something, rather they act as *reinforcement*. Words and action are saying the same thing, but in two different ways.

Thirdly, words and symbols may be used for *subversion* of each other. To light a candle after saying 'The world is full of darkness and despair' puts two contrasting things side by side and sets up a new relationship between them. The same effect would come from the singing of *Thine be the Glory* at a

Christian funeral as the coffin is being carried out at the end. Using the *Nunc Dimittis* would be merely reinforcement.

An understanding of the ways words work with symbols can help us to be more creative than this

So when we are announcing or using symbols, it is helpful to use words carefully. Only ever to say, for example 'We drop these stones into the water to remind us that our sins are buried with Jesus' can begin to feel a little crass after a while. An understanding of the ways words work with symbols can help us to be more creative than this.

What Might Help?

Peter and I were running a training week for newly-ordained clergy in a northern diocese, looking at 'Creative Liturgy.' We divided the group into half a dozen small teams, and gave each of them a season of the year and a service (Eucharist, Evening Prayer and so on) and asked them to construct an act of worship for that season, which we would use for our worship later in the week. It so happened that the group responsible for Advent was composed entirely of women.

When we came to that service, the first thing we noticed was that the worship space had been swathed in yards of purple cloth (the colour for Advent). I remember wondering where they had got it from, even questioning whether women always travelled everywhere with a few bolts just in case they might get called on to run an Advent service. Later on during the service we were invited to use water as a symbol of cleansing and penitence. Water was placed in a large metal bowl (I think they got that from the kitchen) and we were to go forward and be sprinkled with the water. When it was my turn, I was deeply moved to notice floating in the water a single small purple flower. I could not help but think that that would never have occurred to a man! Yet it was a little touch which provided the difference between a purely functional piece of equipment and a thing of beauty.

It was a little touch which provided the difference between a purely functional piece of equipment and a thing of beauty

So having decided what we're going to do, how and where we'll do it, what we'll need and how the logistics will work, the next question is to ask if there are any of these little touches which will make it even more special. Background music, lighting, colour and so on can, as we discussed earlier, create atmosphere. Like art itself these things are not essential to life, but they really do enrich it if handled well. You may like to make sure there are some women on the team!

> ## For Discussion
>
> How much attention do you think is given in your church to the little touches which can make so much difference?
>
> Is there anything you might do to raise people's awareness of the importance of this, and to think more carefully about things which could add value to your worship?

How Will It End?

We have started, but how do we finish? The way we wrap up a part of the service where people are invited to do something, and the way we move on to the next part, is another one of those little touches which, unless it is given careful thought, can spoil the whole. I think the essence of moving on has to do with regathering—often any response people are invited to make will be a personal and individual one, and if we have handled it well we will have helped create for people a bit of space and time for them to encounter God one-to-one. In order to move on we need to remind people that we are a corporate body of people as well as a group of individuals, and that our continuing worship is to be offered together as well as personally. So I often end with a prayer, a liturgical response or a hymn or song which has the effect of bringing people back together. Obviously what we say or sing at this point will be that which gathers us and our individual encounters with God, just as a collect traditionally 'collects' together the individual prayers of the worshippers. To round off a time of action in this way can make a service of worship seem more like a flowing whole than a list of items on an agenda which we have to get through before the blessing.

It is worth saying a word about clearing up here. Be careful not to undo or reverse the symbolism for people by insensitive removal of materials too quickly after the service. Stones laid at the foot of a cross, for example, may represent deeply personal matters, and it can be most upsetting to see them shovelled unceremoniously into a rubbish bin immediately after the service, or even to hear children giggling with one another about what is written on them.

Two contrasting services make this point. At one we were all fired up by a rip-roaring sermon to go out and spread the light of Christ in a dark world, and were all given lighted baptism candles. The instruction 'Now let's all blow out our candles and share the Peace' seemed to have a rather unfortunate symbolism to it. At another service, though, candles were distributed at the end, and we were encouraged to leave the church and let the wind blow them out, just as the wind of the Spirit would scatter us from our place of gathering to different parts of the city. At the end of the day the candles did have to be blown out, but the way it was handled could either negate or reinforce the point of having lit them in the first place.

How Did It Go?

The importance of some kind of review is vital if we are to grow and learn, but it is the most frequent thing to get left out in church circles. As well as listening for individual stories and reactions from members of the congregation, wise leaders will take some time to sit down and talk about how they felt the service went. One helpful way to do this is the 'A B C D' model.

> 'A' stands for 'affirm' — what did we do well, what did we get right? What would we do exactly the same if we did something similar again?
>
> 'B' stands for 'better' — what was OK, but with hindsight could have been improved had we thought of so and so? Listen and learn!
>
> 'C' stands for 'create' — what might we do next time which we did not do this time? What lessons have we learnt which will enable us to do something new in the future?
>
> 'D' stands for 'drop' — what do we wish we had not done, and would never ever do again at any cost?

Another helpful piece of wisdom is the 'Sunday—Wednesday' rule. When reviewing individuals' 'performances' as opposed to the concept as a whole, it is helpful to say positive things to them straight away, but to leave any negative comments until after Wednesday. To have been up in front of a congregation can be, even for experienced worship-leaders, a harrowing experience. If things have not gone well leaders are generally only too well-aware of it — the last thing they need is your helpful advice. So allow a few days for recovery and a longer perspective, and then gently offer some constructive criticism.

For Discussion

What opportunities are there in your church for feedback and review of worship (or indeed of any other aspects of your life)?

How might you set up such opportunities?[5]

5

How To Get It Wrong

Having tried to explain some principles for good practice, it may help to end with the opposite—some errors to avoid in the use of symbol and action.

For Discussion

Have you ever experienced symbol or action in worship which didn't quite work? How did it leave you feeling?

Share some horror stories in the group before you go on and read mine.

Here are four principles gleaned from some of my own bad experiences and personal mistakes.

Don't Overdo It

Whilst I have argued that action has been a missing piece from the great jigsaw of worship for many years, we need to remember it is not the only piece. I have tried to emphasize that words are still important and useful, as are music and silence. What we are after is not a pendulum swing back in the direction of the symbolic, but a right and helpful balance between all the possibilities in worship.

The key, it seems to me, is 'appropriateness.' Given the theme and aim for this service, would it help to invite people to *do* something? If it would, then do it, but if not, don't. In fact I dream of worship where this principle is applied to *all* the elements—would it help to have a choir anthem, or any hymns, or a sermon, on this particular occasion? If not, then why on earth are we doing it? I am sure there are some things which it is always necessary to include, but probably not as many as some of our service books seem to suggest.

> *The key, it seems to me, is 'appropriateness'*

Another way of overdoing it is to limit the kinds of response of which we make use. I can remember my wife despairing at some published Children's Group material a few years ago. They were following the story of Moses, and it started well. They looked at his birth and God's protection of him, and the children were then given bulrush-shaped pieces of card on which they could write or draw prayers. These they then stuck onto a frieze. The next week they learnt about the oppression of the Hebrew slaves by the Egyptians. In response they were invited to write prayers onto bits of card in the shape of bricks, and stick them onto a frieze. The next week—you have guessed it—they wrote prayers on bits of card the shape of manna (whatever shape that is). I think that was the point at which Chris gave up and wrote her own material, just before writing prayers on card in the shape of stone tablets. (You will be glad to know they tiptoed quietly past the paragraph about Zipporah and her son's foreskin.)

A church moving in the direction of symbol and action will want to move past lighting tea-lights and dropping stones into water—again the question is to do with appropriateness. It is easy to go so far and become stuck. The questions with which we began, to do with turning the Bible's metaphors into actions, can help us to be creative rather than predictable.

Don't Do It For the Sake of It

This is a similar point, but it is worth making. It is possible for churches to begin to think that they have to build in some active response time at every single service. Thus the driving question becomes 'Where can we fit this in?' rather than 'What might it be appropriate to fit in?' Response time begins to take on a liturgical feel, and is done because 'we always do it that way.' So inevitably impact is lost, and there is nothing held in reserve for those special times when it would be particularly helpful. There is a delicate balance between the need to worship with more than just words and the routinization of what should be a special and significant part of our worship.

Inevitably impact is lost, and there is nothing held n reserve for those special times when it would be particularly helpful

Don't Do It Pointlessly

I can remember being a speaker at a conference a few years back. It was a charismatic do, largely run by non-Anglicans, but the first signs of the now epidemic boredom with the worship-song culture were beginning to show, so the organizers were beginning to explore some richer ways of worshipping, through the symbolic. Had they asked a proper liturgist to help, things might have gone better, but it quickly became clear that no-one had the first idea what they were doing or, more importantly, why.

During one session the space at the front of the huge conference hall had spread across it large pieces of brightly coloured cloth, each perhaps six metres long and a couple wide. At a particular point in the proceedings we were invited to come forward and stand on whichever piece of cloth felt the most appropriate for us. As an Anglican priest I headed straight for the purple bit, of course, and dutifully stood there. No explanation had been given as to why we had been asked to move, what the purpose or significance of the action was, or what we were supposed to do now we were there, so we all stood there like lemons for a while before eventually drifting back to our seats. The leadership on the stage reverted to charismatic default mode and we sang another song. The whole experience left me asking the question 'Why?', which is incidentally a very good question to ask often about all sorts of the things leaders get us to do during worship.

No explanation had been given as to why we had been asked to move, so we all stood there like lemons

Don't Do It Counter-productively

At another conference recently I was sitting in the front row for the final communion service. While people were receiving bread and wine, we were told, there were a few creative prayer options for us. There were the usual candles and stones and things, but I was particularly interested in two of the stations. On a table at the back were some sheets of paper and felt-tip pens, and a couple of those office shredders which are now essential household accessories due to the rise of identity theft. We could go and write a prayer on the paper, we were told, and then go and put it through the shredder. This symbolism seemed not just a bit daft, but actually quite distressing to me personally, since, without boring you with the details, our family had just lived through a two year period when it felt as though every single prayer we prayed went straight into God's shredder without him even bothering to read it. All the misery and distress of those years came flooding back to me. By all means write some sins you want to confess, maybe the ones which are too serious and private even to leave around the church written on a stone, and shred them as an act of penitence, but not prayers. The symbolism was all wrong.

Distressing in a different way was another prayer station which consisted of a large tree log, a pile of nails and a couple of hammers. While the communion was going on, we could, if we wished, come and hammer a nail into the log 'as a sign of prayer.' (Why?) Imagine the scene. People reverently receiving bread and wine at the front, a small worship band playing quiet ersatz-Celtic worship songs, the occasional whirr of a shredder from the back, and the gentle sound of nails being whacked into a log, with a muttered expletive now and then as people hit their thumbs instead of the nails. The log happened to be directly in front of where I was sitting, with my son next to me, and we watched as (sorry if I appear sexist; I am merely reporting the incident) several women tried in vain to get the nails in without bending them, sending them spinning across the floor or missing entirely. After a while my son whispered to me 'Do you really think Jesus, who, you will remember, trained as a carpenter, is actually enjoying *this* as an act of worship to him?'

Nice ideas, but not properly thought out and not connected in any way to the theme of the service. The sense of distress at the shredders and the mirth at the hammering served between them to kill any sense of worship for me. It would have been better not to have bothered as far as I was concerned.

The sense of distress at the shredders and the mirth at the hammering served between them to kill any sense of worship for me

6 Clashing Symbols?

I do not know how reading this book has made you feel, particularly if you are a church leader looking to move forward in your worship.

I guess that in some churches the very idea that you might start sloshing water around or eating things during the service feels like a complete non-starter. Indeed in some churches the very notion that you might get people to *do* anything seems an impossible one. If that is how you are feeling, let me end with a brief word of encouragement.

I have been trying for some years now to put into practice the principles in this book. In fact most of the examples I have given are from services that I have planned and led. I have tried to involve symbol and action both in my own churches when I was a vicar, and in churches I visited in the course of itinerant work. I can honestly say that in neither scenario have I received serious negative reactions from people. I have tried to set up response activities sensitively, and never to force people into doing anything with which they felt uncomfortable. I have of course had people who did not respond, but that is fine, as I have explained earlier. I have also had one or two traditional charismatics who wanted to stop messing around and get back to singing worship-songs. But generally speaking those whom I would have expected to resist anything new have welcomed the opportunity to respond to God in some different ways.

A memory which I will take to my grave with me was of a Good Friday service when we were thinking about the grain of wheat which must fall to the ground and die so that new fruit could grow. Everyone was given a pea seed as they arrived, and later on in the service they were encouraged to think about what in their lives they would like to die, so that greater fruit could result. At the front of the church were several seed-trays full of soil, and as a response people were invited, if they wanted to, to come and plant their seed into the soil. One of the congregation was an elderly gentleman who had resisted me every step of the way in my ministry. He was a traditional eight o'clock communion Anglican, and he had let me know many times how much he disliked what I was doing to his church. But on this occasion he was one of the first to come up, and I could see from his face that something in the service had moved him deeply. The moment of his planting his seed remains in my mind as an icon of even the hardest hearts being melted by the right kind of creative liturgy. If he was happy with it, pretty much everybody else would be.

The end of the story, by the way, is that on Easter Sunday people arrived in church to find seed trays of sprouting plants (here's one I made earlier!) as the new growth, made possible by Jesus' resurrection, was beginning to show.

I believe that people of all ages, sorts and conditions are ready for more active worship which uses more than just words. If you have any responsibility for worship in your church, I would encourage you to go for it. I hope this book has given you a clear enough guide to help you, and I believe you will be pleasantly surprised at the result.

For Discussion

In the light of what you have learnt from this book, what steps might you begin to take in making your worship more multisensory?

How practically are you going to go about this?

7 Resources

There are two kinds of material on this subject, some which provides the theoretical background and some which give you off-the-peg ideas.

Theory:
- Peter Craig-Wild, *Tools for Transformation* (London: DLT, 2002)
- Tim Lomax and Michael Moynagh, *Liquid Worship* (Grove Worship booklet W 181)
- Pete Ward, *Liquid Church* (Carlisle: Paternoster, 2002)

Practice:
- Andy Flannagan, *Distinctive Worship* (Milton Keynes: Spring Harvest, 2004)(See also www.youthwork.co.uk/resources)
- Chris Leach, *100 Worship Activities* (Eastbourne: Kingsway, 2000)
- Tim Lomax, *Freedom within a Framework* (Buxhall: Kevin Mayhew, 2001)
- Tim Lomax, *More Freedom within a Framework* (Buxhall: Kevin Mayhew, 2002)
- Ian Tarrant and Sally Dakin, *Labyrinths and Prayer Stations* (Grove Worship booklet W 180)
- Sue Wallace, *Multisensory Prayer* (Milton Keynes: SU, 2000)
- Sue Wallace, *Multisensory Church* (Milton Keynes: SU, 2002)

Notes

1   P Craig-Wild, *Tools for Transformation* (London: DLT, 2002)

2   The classic example of this risk is the story of Nehushtan, the bronze serpent through which the Israelites were healed of snake bites, which later became an object of idolatrous worship. See Num 21:8–9 and 2 Kings 18:4.

3   It is in fact a biblical principle that too low a temperature will hinder evangelism—Paul tells us in 1 Cor 1:18 that 'the message of the cross is foolishness to those who are perishing.'

4   See my *Responding to Preaching* (Grove Worship booklet W 139)

5   See my *Leading Worship that Connects* (Eastbourne: Kingsway, 1999) p 61ff for details of a scheme I used in my parish.